chardonnay moms

chardonnay moms

Jane and Bobbi's greatest hits.
Our favorites from more than a decade
of newspaper, online, and calendar cartoons.

Here's to ALL the
Pinot Grigio
Cabernet
Merlot
Sauvignon Blanc
and especially Chardonnay Moms!

cheers!

To Ken, Todd and Mac.
My best audience.
Love you with every laugh in my body.
Jane

To Steve, Mary Ann, Madison, Hunter, Sean and Chad
who have brought more joy and laughter into my life
than they'll ever know. I love you.
Bobbi

And to all our friends in Greenwich, CT
who've been enjoying our cartoons,
putting them on their refrigerators,
and supporting us for so many years.
We love you, too.

"When all else fails, try chardonnay."

"Life is good.
I start each day with a latte
and end with a chardonnay."

"Hello, Yale?
I'd like Prenatal Admissions, please."

"I can't think without my bra on."

"My kids are all buying me gifts for Father's Day.
I hope I can afford it."

"I spent 90% of my money on wine and women.
The rest? Wasted."

"Ever notice, the bigger the house,
the less the wife weighs?"

"It's spring break, honey.
Just you, me and the kids.
No email, no cell phones, no laptops."

"What's a collect call?"

Born To Drive

"A game without coffee
is like baseball without a bat."

"Your kid just scored a goal. Pretend you saw it!"

"It's spring vacation.
My friends just got back from Aspen.
I just got back from Costco."

"My husband complains
that he never wins any arguments.
That's because he's never right."

"Look at me. It's gluten-free."

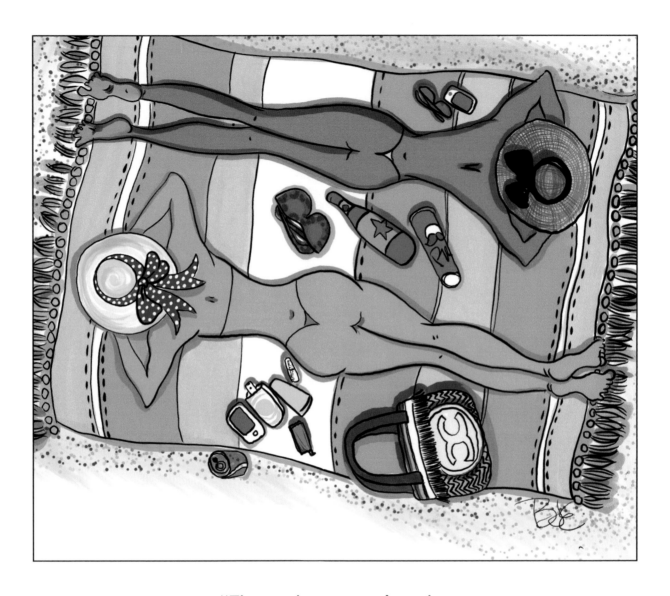

"The rules are simple:
tanning before tequila."

"Give me rich girl hair."

"Someone called you last week. I don't remember
who, and I don't remember exactly when,
but they said it was really important."

"The only thing I like about winter is cashmere."

"A new survey says people who drink
have a lower incidence of dementia."

"I told my colorist to make my hair
the color of champagne."

"*Please* don't make me go to another fundraiser."

"Men fantasize about sex.
Women fantasize about live-in help."

I'm in the will.   I'm out of the will.   I'm back in the will.

"Sure I'm a math nerd now, but she'll be crazy about me when I'm a hedge fund trader."

"I have to go back to work."

"Some people do yoga. I prefer a good cabernet."

"If I spent as much money on myself as my husband spends on his boat, I'd be beautiful, too."

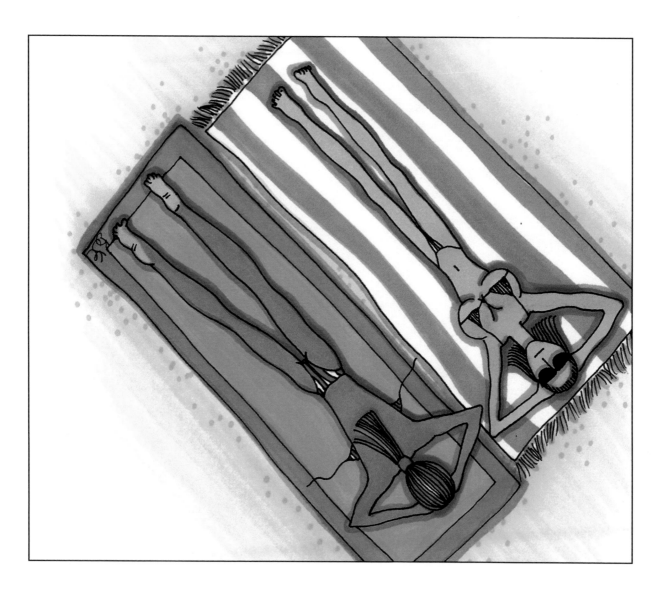

"Nancy, weren't you a chemistry major?
What's the boiling point of silicone?"

"I figure that after buying the plants, fertilizer, topsoil, deer fencing, plus hours of weeding, each tomato costs me $500."

"Remember when phones
were attached to the wall?"

"Any idea how exhausting it is
being nice ALL DAY LONG?"

"You're charging me for emotional baggage?!"

"I'd like to tutor your son this summer,
but your house doesn't have a pool."

"Lunch?"

"Bruce, at my age, THONG rhymes with WRONG."

"Investment club, book group, auction meeting...
it's just another reason to drink wine."

"Some of my friends tell me I'm ADD.
I prefer to think I'm just enthusiastic!"

"I packed my son's camp trunk
with ten pairs of underpants. He came back
with nine pairs, still folded, in the exact same spot."

"Red or white
should be the biggest decision of my day."

"Everyone's at rehab. I want to get away, too."

"Today I have style. Tomorrow I'll have a startup."

"I love class coffees.
I get to check out other people's houses."

"I need a wife."

"We've been married a long time.
Our guest bedroom is now his snoring room."

"There is joy in aging when you can't remember
your third wife's name."

"We always have so much to talk about.
The games keep interrupting us."

"Trick or treat.
I'm the princess and he's my lawyer."

"Mom! Stop eating my Halloween candy!
I can hear you opening the candy wrappers."

"Don't badmouth Halloween.
It's the family business."

"Same sex marriage? What's the problem?
My husband and I have been having
the same sex for years."

"I need to have a fundraising party...
to fundraise for *ME*."

"I traded *Sex in the City*
for *Hockey in the Suburbs.*"

"We may have lost but we had the best snacks."

"Hello Princeton? I'm the new wife.
How does that legacy thing work?"

"I'm not prejudiced. I hate everyone."

"My colorist or my husband?
Don't make me choose."

"When I was pregnant with you,
I read *What to Expect When You're Expecting*,
but this wasn't it."

"I'm tired of being the parent.
I want to be the kid."

"The only good thing about menopause
is that it helps me get in touch with my inner bitch."

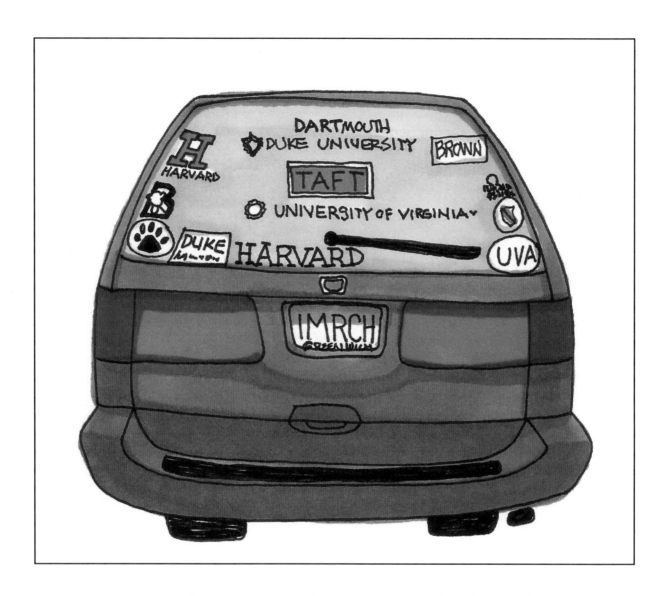

"I'm not impressed. All I see is tuition bills."

"Grandpa's very sick, dear.
Now go in there and ask him his PIN numbers."

"Honey, I'm home and I saved you
$2,000 at the outlets!"

"I need a cup of coffee before I can decide
what kind of coffee I want."

"We'd love to have Thanksgiving with you.
But Black Friday stores are opening early this year."

"You're kidding, right?"

"I like to think of myself as a Neiman Marxist."

"Yeah, like those are real."

Perception

Reality

"I have a kid I'd like to re-gift."

"It's 6:00.
I made it through another day.
Here's to me!"